Biography Mayweather

The Unbeaten Legacy of a Boxing Icon

Curtis Hermes

Copyright © 2025 Curtis Hermes

All rights reserved.

No part of this book may be reproduced, stored in a retrieval system, or transmitted in any form or by any means, electronic, mechanical, photocopying, recording, or otherwise, without the prior written permission of the publisher, except for the use of brief quotations in a book review

Printed in Dunstable, United Kingdom

Table Of Contents

Introduction	6
Chapter 1: The Making of a Champion	**9**
Early Life in Grand Rapids	9
A Family of Fighters: The Mayweather Legacy	12
The Olympic Dream and Turning Pro	15
Chapter 2: The Rise to Stardom	**17**
Dominating the Lower Weight Classes	17
The Birth of "Pretty Boy" Floyd	20
Key Early Fights and First World Title	23
Chapter 3: The Transformation into "Money" Mayweather	**28**
Reinventing Himself: From Pretty Boy to Money	28
The Business of Boxing: Taking Control of His Career	32
The Move to Pay-Per-View Superstar	34
Chapter 4: Defensive Genius – The Art of Not Getting Hit	**40**
The Shoulder Roll and Mastering Defense	40
Ring IQ: Outsmarting Opponents	44
Training Regimen: Work Ethic and Dedication	48
Chapter 5: The Biggest Fights of His Career	**54**
Mayweather vs. Oscar De La Hoya – The Fight That Changed Everything	55

    The Undefeated Rivalry: Cotto, Mosley, and Others   58

    The Superfight: Mayweather vs. Pacquiao   61

Chapter 6: Controversies and Criticism   65

    Inside and Outside the Ring: Legal Issues and Personal Life   67

    Public Perception: Arrogance vs. Confidence   70

    The Debate Over His Fighting Style   73

Chapter 7: The Business of Floyd Mayweather   78

    Building the Mayweather Brand   79

    Money Moves: How He Became Boxing's First Billionaire   82

    The Legacy of The Money Team (TMT)   86

Chapter 8: Life Beyond Boxing   91

    Retirement Announcements and Comebacks   93

    Exhibition Fights and Staying Relevant   96

    Business Ventures and Investments   99

Chapter 9: Mayweather's Legacy in Boxing   105

    How He Changed the Sport Financially and Technically   106

    Comparing Mayweather to Boxing's All-Time Greats   110

    Influence on the Next Generation of Fighters   115

Chapter 10: What It Means to Be Undefeated   119

    The Mentality of a Champion   120

    The Price of Perfection: Sacrifices and Discipline   123

    Lessons from Mayweather's Career   127

Introduction

What does it take to be truly undefeated? Is it sheer talent, relentless discipline, or an unbreakable mindset? In the world of boxing, where legends are made and broken in a matter of seconds, few names command as much respect—and controversy—as Floyd Mayweather. With an unblemished 50-0 record, Mayweather isn't just a boxer; he's a phenomenon, a businessman, and a cultural icon who redefined the sport both inside and outside the ring.

This book will take a deep dive into Mayweather's journey, from his humble beginnings in Grand Rapids, Michigan, to becoming the highest-paid athlete of his time. We'll explore the grueling training regimens, the calculated strategies, and the personal and professional rivalries that shaped his career. Beyond the sport, we'll analyze his impact on boxing's financial structure, his persona as "Money Mayweather," and the controversies that often surrounded him.

More than just a biography, this is a study of what it means to dominate a field with an unwavering commitment to success. How did Mayweather turn himself into a billion-dollar brand? What lessons can be drawn from his defensive mastery, his psychological warfare, and his ability to control the narrative? Whether you admire him, despise him, or find yourself somewhere in between, one thing is certain: Floyd Mayweather is a name that cannot be ignored.

As we unravel his story, we'll seek to answer a larger question—what does it truly mean to be the best?

Chapter 1: The Making of a Champion

Early Life in Grand Rapids

Floyd Joy Mayweather Jr. He came into the world on February 24, 1977, in Grand Rapids, Michigan. From the moment he could walk, boxing was a part of his life. His father, Floyd Mayweather Sr., was a professional boxer who once fought Sugar Ray Leonard, and his uncles, Roger and Jeff Mayweather, were also accomplished fighters. The sport ran through his blood, shaping his childhood in ways few can imagine.

But while his upbringing revolved around boxing, it was far from an easy life. Mayweather grew up in a tough neighborhood where poverty and crime were part of the daily reality. His mother, Deborah Sinclair, struggled with addiction, and his father was frequently absent due to his own boxing career and later, incarceration. As a child, Floyd often found himself living with his grandmother, who became one of his biggest supporters.

Despite the hardships, one thing remained constant—his dedication to boxing. His father had him training at an early age, molding him into a disciplined fighter. Even in his teenage years, Mayweather's focus was unparalleled. He spent countless hours in the gym, refining his skills, developing his speed, and perfecting his defensive technique.

His early years in Grand Rapids were marked by struggle, but they also built the foundation for his relentless work ethic. Unlike other kids, Floyd didn't have time for distractions—his world revolved around the ring.

A Family of Fighters: The Mayweather Legacy

Mayweather didn't just grow up around boxing—he was born into a dynasty of fighters. His father, Floyd Sr., was known for his defensive skill, but his uncles played just as significant a role in shaping his career.

Roger Mayweather, who would later become Floyd Jr.'s longtime trainer, was a two-time world champion. Known as the "Black Mamba," Roger brought experience and wisdom to Floyd's training, ensuring that he learned not just the art of hitting but the equally important art of not getting hit.

Jeff Mayweather, another uncle, was a former fighter who later turned to coaching. While he wasn't as prominent as Roger, his influence was still part of Floyd's development. This deep-rooted boxing heritage gave Mayweather a competitive edge—he wasn't just trained by coaches; he was mentored by a family of champions.

However, the Mayweather family wasn't without its conflicts. Floyd Sr. was a strict, often harsh trainer, and his relationship with his son was filled with tension. When Floyd Sr. went to prison for drug trafficking, Roger took over as his trainer, which caused further division between father and son. Despite their rocky relationship, Floyd Jr. inherited his father's defensive instincts and technical mastery.

The Mayweather legacy was both a blessing and a challenge. On one hand, it gave Floyd an unmatched level of knowledge and training; on the other, it created intense family dynamics that would follow him throughout his career.

The Olympic Dream and Turning Pro

Mayweather's amateur career was nothing short of spectacular. He compiled an impressive record of 84 wins and only 8 losses, showcasing his immense talent on the national stage. By the time he was selected to represent the United States at the 1996 Olympics in Atlanta, he was already regarded as one of the best amateur boxers in the world.

At the Olympics, Mayweather competed in the featherweight division. He displayed his signature defensive style and quick counterpunching, advancing through the tournament with ease. However, controversy struck in the semifinals when he lost a highly disputed decision to Bulgaria's Serafim Todorov. Many believed

Mayweather had clearly won the fight, but the judges awarded the bout to Todorov. The loss denied Mayweather a gold medal, leaving him with a bronze—a result that didn't sit well with him.

Despite the disappointment, the Olympics proved that Mayweather was ready for the professional ranks. He turned pro later that year, making his debut against Roberto Apodaca in October 1996. It was a one-sided affair—Mayweather dominated and won by knockout in the second round.

From that moment, it was clear that Mayweather was destined for greatness. His professional career started with a blend of speed, precision, and defensive mastery, setting the stage for what would become one of the most legendary boxing careers of all time.

Chapter 2: The Rise to Stardom

Dominating the Lower Weight Classes

Floyd Mayweather Jr. entered the professional boxing world with a reputation as a polished, technically gifted fighter. After an impressive amateur career that included an Olympic bronze medal, Mayweather wasted no time making an impact in the lower weight divisions. Fighting in the super featherweight (130 lbs) division, he displayed remarkable speed, precision, and defensive skills—qualities that would define his legendary career.

From his debut in 1996, it became clear that Mayweather was not just another promising prospect; he was a fighter with world-class potential. Under the guidance of his uncle Roger Mayweather, Floyd perfected the "shoulder roll" defensive technique, a style that allowed him to deflect punches while counterattacking with sharp, accurate shots. His ability to avoid damage while delivering precise combinations made him nearly untouchable.

His early fights were a showcase of pure talent. Mayweather moved through his opponents with ease, often overwhelming them with a mix of speed and power. He won his first 17 fights, most by knockout, and it was evident that he was ready for a title shot.

In 1998, just two years after turning professional, Mayweather faced Genaro Hernández for the WBC super featherweight title. Hernández was an experienced champion who had only lost once in his career—to the legendary Oscar De La Hoya. Many believed this would be a difficult test for the young Mayweather, but Floyd dominated the fight from start to finish. His superior speed and reflexes allowed him to control every round, forcing Hernández's corner to stop the fight after the eighth round. At just 21 years old, Mayweather had become a world champion, marking the beginning of his reign in the lower weight classes.

The Birth of "Pretty Boy" Floyd

With his rise in the boxing world, Mayweather quickly developed an image that set him apart from other fighters. He was fast, flashy, and confident—attributes that earned him the nickname "Pretty Boy" Floyd. Unlike many boxers who bore the scars of their battles, Mayweather's impeccable defense kept his face unmarked. His clean-cut appearance and brash personality made him a rising star both in and out of the ring.

Mayweather's confidence was backed up by his performances. His defensive mastery made it almost impossible for opponents to land clean shots, frustrating even the most skilled challengers. As he continued to dominate, he embraced his new persona, showing an increasing level of swagger in pre-fight interviews and press conferences. He was a fighter who knew he was special, and he wasn't afraid to say it.

During this time, Mayweather also made strategic business moves that would later define his career. He understood the value of marketing and the importance of building a brand. His fights became more than just sporting events—they were spectacles. He took inspiration from fighters like Muhammad Ali, using trash talk and bold predictions to generate buzz.

Outside the ring, Mayweather's persona began to evolve. He surrounded himself with luxury, flaunting designer clothes, expensive cars, and diamond-encrusted jewelry. He was still a young fighter climbing the ranks, but he carried himself like a superstar.

As his undefeated streak continued, so did the attention. Mayweather wasn't just another champion—he was quickly becoming one of the biggest names in boxing. His blend of talent, charisma, and showmanship made him a must-watch fighter, and the boxing world took notice.

Key Early Fights and First World Title

After winning his first world title against Genaro Hernández, Mayweather continued his dominance in the super featherweight division. Each fight was a display of technical brilliance, reinforcing his reputation as one of the best pound-for-pound fighters in the world.

One of his early defining moments came in 1999 when he defended his WBC title against Diego Corrales. At the time, Corrales was an undefeated knockout artist with a reputation for devastating power. Many believed this would be Mayweather's toughest test yet. However, what followed was one of the most one-sided performances in boxing history.

From the opening bell, Mayweather's speed and precision were too much for Corrales. He picked his shots carefully, landing clean punches while avoiding Corrales' powerful swings. Round after round, Corrales struggled to touch him. By the time the fight was stopped in the tenth round, Mayweather had knocked Corrales down five times, cementing his status as a generational talent.

Following this dominant performance, Mayweather continued his reign by defending his title against tough challengers, including Carlos Hernández and Jesús Chávez. With each victory, he solidified his place as the king of the division.

However, Mayweather wasn't content with just one weight class. Like all great fighters, he wanted to test himself against bigger opponents and claim championships in multiple divisions. In 2002, he made the decision to move up to the lightweight division (135 lbs), setting his sights on new challenges.

His first fight at lightweight was against José Luis Castillo for the WBC title. This was a major step up in competition—Castillo was a physically strong, pressure-fighting champion known for his relentless attack. Unlike Mayweather's previous fights, this bout was highly competitive. Castillo was able to land punches on Floyd, something few had done before. In the end, Mayweather secured a controversial unanimous decision victory, but many believed Castillo had done enough to win.

To remove any doubt, Mayweather granted Castillo an immediate rematch. This time, he put on a more convincing performance, using his superior footwork and ring IQ to secure a clear decision win. With this victory, Mayweather had become a two-division world champion, proving that his skills translated to higher weight classes.

His rise to stardom was now undeniable. He had dominated the super featherweight division and was beginning to establish himself as a force at lightweight. His ability to move up in weight while maintaining his defensive brilliance and speed was a rare feat, showcasing his versatility as a fighter.

By the early 2000s, Floyd Mayweather Jr. was no longer just a promising young fighter—he was a bona fide star. The combination of his undefeated record, flashy persona, and growing dominance made him one of the most talked-about figures in the sport. But as his career progressed, bigger challenges awaited, and Mayweather was determined to prove that he was not just great—but the greatest of all time.

Chapter 3: The Transformation into "Money" Mayweather

Reinventing Himself: From Pretty Boy to Money

Floyd Mayweather Jr. had already established himself as one of the best fighters in the sport under the "Pretty Boy" moniker, but as he moved further into his career, he realized that being the best inside the ring was not enough. Boxing was not just a sport—it was a business. The name "Pretty Boy" had served him well in the early stages of his career, but it did not reflect the magnitude of the empire he was building. He needed a new identity—one that signified power, wealth, and total control. Thus, "Money" Mayweather was born.

The shift from "Pretty Boy" to "Money" Mayweather was not just about branding; it was a complete transformation of his approach to boxing and his public persona. Mayweather leaned into the excesses of wealth, flaunting stacks of cash, expensive jewelry, luxury cars, and private jets. He wanted the world to see him as more than just an athlete—he was a businessman, an entertainer, and a marketing genius.

This transformation also reflected his understanding of the entertainment industry. He realized that the most financially successful fighters were not just the most skilled but also the most marketable. He studied the careers of legends like Muhammad Ali and Sugar Ray Leonard, both of whom used charisma, showmanship, and psychological warfare to elevate their fights into must-watch events. Mayweather took it a step further, embracing the role of the villain in the boxing world.

He openly bragged about his wealth, dismissed his opponents as inferior, and turned every pre-fight press conference into a spectacle. He understood that fans would pay just as much to see him lose as they would to see him win. By playing the role of the brash, arrogant, and undefeated champion, he guaranteed that every fight he participated in would be a major financial success.

However, this transformation was not just for show. It symbolized his complete control over his destiny. No longer just a fighter, he was now the architect of his career, making moves that would cement his legacy both inside and outside the ring.

The Business of Boxing: Taking Control of His Career

One of the most pivotal moments in Mayweather's career came in 2006 when he made a decision that would change his financial future forever—he bought out his contract with Top Rank Promotions for $750,000. At the time, this move seemed risky. Top Rank, led by Bob Arum, had guided his career and helped him become a world champion. However, Mayweather knew that if he truly wanted to maximize his earnings and have full control over his fights, he had to break free from traditional boxing promoters.

By becoming his own promoter under Mayweather Promotions, he eliminated the middlemen who took large portions of fighters' earnings. He no longer had to split his purse with a promoter who dictated his career moves. Instead, he negotiated his own deals, handpicked his fights, and ensured that he received the lion's share of every event's revenue.

This decision put him in a rare position of power in the boxing world. Historically, promoters controlled the sport, dictating matchups and collecting significant portions of a fighter's earnings. Mayweather flipped the script. He showed that fighters, if smart and strategic, could take control of their own financial destinies.

One of his first major tests as a self-promoted fighter was his bout against Oscar De La Hoya in 2007. This fight was Mayweather's first major pay-per-view event and would determine whether he could truly thrive without the backing of a major promotional company.

The Move to Pay-Per-View Superstar

Mayweather's fight against Oscar De La Hoya was a defining moment, not just for his career but for the business of boxing itself. De La Hoya was already a crossover star, one of the most popular and marketable boxers of his era. Mayweather understood that this fight was his chance to elevate himself from a great fighter to a global superstar.

The buildup to the fight was unlike anything boxing had seen in years. Mayweather, now fully embracing his "Money" persona, played the perfect antagonist to De La Hoya's golden-boy image. The press conferences were intense, the trash talk was relentless, and

Mayweather made sure to capture as much attention as possible.

The fight itself was highly competitive, but Mayweather's superior skill and defense earned him a split-decision victory. More importantly, the event shattered records, generating 2.4 million pay-per-view buys—at the time, the highest in boxing history. The financial success of the fight proved that Mayweather had made the right decision to leave Top Rank. He earned a reported $25 million from the fight, a figure that would only grow in subsequent years.

After defeating De La Hoya, Mayweather became the face of boxing. Every fight he participated in became a major event, with millions tuning in to see if anyone could finally defeat the undefeated champion. He continued to dominate the sport, defeating top fighters like Ricky Hatton, Juan Manuel Marquez, and Shane Mosley.

By the time he faced Mosley in 2010, Mayweather had mastered the art of pay-per-view promotion. He understood that boxing was no longer just about the fights—it was about selling a story. He created narratives around his bouts, ensuring that every fight felt like a must-watch event.

One of the key aspects of Mayweather's pay-per-view success was his ability to control the revenue streams. He demanded the biggest share of the purse, negotiated deals that gave him a percentage of pay-per-view sales, and ensured that every aspect of fight promotion worked in his favor. His fights routinely generated hundreds of millions of dollars, with

Mayweather taking home record-breaking paychecks.

His strategic business moves culminated in 2015 when he faced Manny Pacquiao in what was dubbed "The Fight of the Century." The bout generated a staggering 4.6 million pay-per-view buys and grossed over $600 million, making it the most lucrative fight in boxing history. Mayweather walked away with an estimated $250 million payday—proof that he had completely mastered the business of boxing.

At this point, Mayweather had fully transformed into "Money" Mayweather, the highest-paid athlete in the world and an unstoppable force in the fight game. His business acumen had allowed him to rewrite the rules of the sport, setting a new standard for how fighters could control their careers and financial futures.

Conclusion

The transformation from "Pretty Boy" Floyd to "Money" Mayweather was far more than a name change—it was a calculated, strategic evolution that allowed Mayweather to dominate boxing both financially and athletically. He realized that skill alone was not enough; fighters needed to understand the business side of the sport to truly thrive. By taking control of his career, promoting himself, and turning his fights into global spectacles, Mayweather became more than just a champion—he became an empire.

His success paved the way for future generations of fighters, showing them that they could demand more control over their earnings and brand themselves as more than just athletes. Mayweather's approach to business, promotion, and entertainment redefined what it meant to be a superstar in boxing, ensuring that his legacy would extend far beyond his undefeated record.

With "Money" Mayweather at the helm, boxing was no longer just about winning titles—it was about changing the game itself.

Chapter 4: Defensive Genius – The Art of Not Getting Hit

The Shoulder Roll and Mastering Defense

Boxing has always been defined by the brutal nature of its exchanges. Fighters often go into the ring knowing they will take punishment in pursuit of victory. However, Floyd Mayweather Jr. defied this conventional wisdom by perfecting a style built on the principle of "hit and don't get hit." At the core of this strategy was his mastery of the shoulder roll defense, a technique that became his signature move and helped him remain undefeated throughout his career.

The shoulder roll is not a new concept in boxing. Fighters like James Toney and Archie Moore used variations of it before Mayweather, but none applied it as effectively and consistently as he did. The technique involves keeping the lead shoulder raised and slightly turned inward, while the rear hand remains close to the chin to deflect punches. This allows a fighter to deflect incoming shots off the shoulder, rolling with punches instead of absorbing them directly.

Mayweather's application of the shoulder roll was nearly flawless. His impeccable reflexes and ability to read his opponents made him almost impossible to hit cleanly. Fighters would throw flurries of punches, only for Mayweather to roll his shoulder, slip to the side, or counter with lightning-fast precision. His defensive prowess frustrated even the most aggressive punchers, turning them from fierce competitors into desperate swing-and-miss fighters by the later rounds.

One of the best examples of his shoulder roll mastery was his 2013 fight against Canelo Álvarez. Canelo, a young and powerful puncher, was expected to pose serious problems for the older Mayweather. However, Mayweather neutralized him with ease, using his defensive brilliance to avoid heavy shots and land crisp counters. Canelo spent 12 rounds swinging at air, unable to land anything significant as Mayweather put on a defensive masterclass.

The key to the effectiveness of the shoulder roll was its combination with other defensive maneuvers. Mayweather didn't rely on just one technique—he blended head movement, footwork, and hand positioning into a seamless system that made him one of the most elusive fighters in history. While offense wins fights, defense ensures longevity, and Mayweather's ability to minimize damage played a crucial role in his long and successful career.

Ring IQ: Outsmarting Opponents

Mayweather's defensive genius was not just a product of physical skill—it was also a testament to his extraordinary ring IQ. He was not just a fighter; he was a strategist who approached every bout like a chess match. His ability to read opponents, adjust on the fly, and exploit weaknesses made him nearly unbeatable.

One of Mayweather's greatest strengths was his adaptability. He never fought the same way twice. Against aggressive brawlers, he used movement and counterpunching to neutralize their power. Against technical boxers, he applied pressure, forcing them into uncomfortable situations. He studied his opponents meticulously before every fight, identifying their habits and weaknesses, then executed game plans with surgical precision.

A prime example of this came in his 2015 fight against Manny Pacquiao. Pacquiao was known for his relentless speed and explosive combinations, which had overwhelmed countless opponents. Many believed his southpaw stance and fast in-and-out movement would give Mayweather trouble. However, Mayweather quickly deciphered Pacquiao's rhythm, controlling the distance with his jab and countering effectively. By mid-fight, Pacquiao was struggling to land anything significant, while Mayweather picked him apart with calculated counters.

Another aspect of Mayweather's ring IQ was his patience. He never rushed into exchanges unless absolutely necessary. He let opponents make mistakes, waited for openings, and capitalized with pinpoint accuracy. His fight against Juan Manuel Márquez in 2009 demonstrated this perfectly. Márquez, a brilliant counterpuncher himself, found himself completely outclassed because Mayweather was simply a step ahead at every turn. He controlled the pace, set traps, and landed at will, making one of the sport's best tacticians look ordinary.

Mayweather's understanding of distance and timing was unparalleled. He controlled the space in the ring with expert precision, keeping opponents at bay while staying in position to counter. His ability to dictate range meant he could land clean shots without exposing himself to unnecessary risks. This level of control frustrated opponents, forcing them to take risks that played right into Mayweather's hands.

Beyond technical adjustments, Mayweather also used psychological warfare to his advantage. His trash talk, confidence, and mind games often got into the heads of his opponents before they even stepped into the ring. Fighters would become overly aggressive, looking to prove a point, only to walk into a carefully orchestrated trap. His ability to manipulate the mental aspect of the sport was just as impressive as his physical talents.

Training Regimen: Work Ethic and Dedication

While Mayweather's defensive skills and ring IQ set him apart, they would not have been possible without his legendary work ethic. He was not just naturally talented—he was one of the hardest-working athletes in the history of sports. His training regimen was relentless, ensuring that he was always in peak condition and ready to execute his strategies flawlessly.

Mayweather's dedication to fitness was evident in his famous "hard work, dedication" mantra. He trained year-round, never allowing himself to fall out of shape. Unlike many fighters who balloon in weight between fights, Mayweather remained disciplined, keeping his body conditioned even when he didn't have a scheduled bout. This allowed him to enter training camps already in peak shape, focusing on refining his skills rather than shedding excess weight.

One of the most well-known aspects of his training was his unconventional workout schedule. Mayweather often trained late at night, sometimes starting his workouts at 2 or 3 AM. His reasoning? While his opponents were sleeping, he was working. This mindset reinforced his belief that he was always a step ahead of the competition.

His workouts included grueling cardiovascular sessions, such as running up to 8 miles a day at a blistering pace. His jump rope routines were legendary, showcasing both his footwork and endurance. He also incorporated an extensive focus on reflex training, using tools like the double-end bag, speed bag, and hand-eye coordination drills to sharpen his defensive instincts.

One of Mayweather's most unique training methods was his infamous sparring sessions. He often engaged in intense, marathon-like sparring rounds, sometimes lasting 20 or 30 minutes without breaks. This method, known as "doghouse rules," pushed fighters to their limits, forcing them to develop mental toughness and endurance. His sparring partners were often world-class fighters themselves, yet they struggled to keep up with Mayweather's pace and precision.

Beyond physical conditioning, Mayweather's diet and lifestyle were just as disciplined. He rarely drank alcohol, stayed away from unhealthy foods, and ensured that his body was always prepared for the demands of a fight. His strict regimen allowed him to maintain his speed, reflexes, and endurance well into his late 30s, a rarity in the sport.

His commitment to training also translated into his preparation for fights. He studied film obsessively, breaking down his opponents' habits frame by frame. He would watch their previous fights multiple times, taking notes on their tendencies and weaknesses. This level of preparation allowed him to enter the ring with supreme confidence, knowing he had already won the battle before the first bell rang.

Conclusion

Floyd Mayweather's ability to avoid damage, outthink his opponents, and maintain peak physical condition made him one of the most dominant fighters in history. His mastery of the shoulder roll, unparalleled ring IQ, and relentless work ethic set him apart from his peers, ensuring his legacy as a defensive genius.

While many fighters rely on power or aggression to win fights, Mayweather proved that intelligence and discipline could be just as effective—if not more so. His ability to control every aspect of a fight, from the psychological battle to the physical exchanges, made him an enigma in the ring. Opponents stepped in hoping to crack his defensive code, only to find themselves frustrated, outclassed, and unable to land clean punches.

His legacy is not just about being undefeated—it is about changing the way boxing is approached. Mayweather showed that defense could be just as exciting as offense, and that a fighter's longevity and success depended on strategy just as much as strength. His influence continues to inspire future generations, proving that the true art of boxing lies not in how hard you hit, but in how well you can avoid getting hit.

Chapter 5: The Biggest Fights of His Career

Floyd Mayweather Jr.'s career is defined by the high-stakes fights that cemented his legacy. While his entire boxing journey was marked by dominance, certain fights stand out as pivotal moments that shaped both his career and the sport itself. From his battle with Oscar De La Hoya, which turned him into a household name, to the long-anticipated clash with Manny Pacquiao, Mayweather built a resume filled with legendary bouts.

Mayweather vs. Oscar De La Hoya – The Fight That Changed Everything

By 2007, Floyd Mayweather had already solidified himself as one of the best pound-for-pound fighters in the world. However, he had yet to cross over into mainstream superstardom. That changed when he faced Oscar De La Hoya on May 5, 2007, in a fight that would transform Mayweather from an elite boxer into a global phenomenon.

At the time, De La Hoya was boxing's biggest star. A six-division world champion with crossover appeal, De La Hoya was a pay-per-view powerhouse. Mayweather, though undefeated, was still growing in popularity and saw this fight as the perfect opportunity to break into the mainstream.

The fight was highly publicized, fueled by Mayweather's trash talk and De La Hoya's status as the golden boy of boxing.

The buildup was intense, with Mayweather playing the villain role to perfection. Their interactions on HBO's 24/7 series—the first-ever boxing reality show leading up to a fight—captivated audiences and set a new standard for boxing promotions. Fans were eager to see whether Mayweather's technical prowess could stand up to De La Hoya's experience and power.

Once the fight began, it was clear Mayweather's defensive mastery would be the key factor. De La Hoya started aggressively, trying to impose his size advantage, but Mayweather's shoulder roll defense and counterpunching kept him in control. As the fight progressed, Mayweather's speed and precision proved too much for De La Hoya. In a closely contested bout, Mayweather won by split decision, securing the WBC light middleweight title.

More importantly, this fight shattered pay-per-view records at the time, generating 2.4 million buys and over $130 million in revenue. It was the moment Mayweather became the face of boxing, marking the birth of the "Money" Mayweather era.

The Undefeated Rivalry: Cotto, Mosley, and Others

After the De La Hoya fight, Mayweather was officially the biggest draw in boxing, but he still had to prove himself against a slew of dangerous opponents. His undefeated record became both his badge of honor and a target, as numerous top fighters lined up to try and hand him his first loss.

One of the toughest tests of Mayweather's career came against Miguel Cotto in 2012. Cotto, a relentless pressure fighter with heavy hands, was the reigning WBA super welterweight champion. Many believed Cotto's power and aggression could trouble Mayweather, and for a few rounds, that was the case. Cotto pushed Mayweather harder than most opponents, bloodying his nose and landing solid punches. However, as always, Mayweather adjusted. He used his superior footwork, head movement, and pinpoint accuracy to pull away in the later rounds, winning by unanimous decision.

Before Cotto, there was Shane Mosley in 2010, a fight remembered for one of the most dangerous moments in Mayweather's career. In the second round, Mosley landed a vicious right hand that buckled Mayweather's knees—one of the few times in his career he was visibly hurt. But what happened next showcased Mayweather's championship mentality. Instead of panicking, he immediately adjusted, controlled the fight, and dominated Mosley for the remaining rounds, proving his resilience.

Other opponents, including Ricky Hatton, Juan Manuel Márquez, and Marcos

Maidana, all had their chances, but Mayweather's superior ring IQ always allowed him to stay one step ahead. With each fight, he further built his legacy as one of the most defensively sound and tactically brilliant fighters in history.

The Superfight: Mayweather vs. Pacquiao

If there was one fight that defined Mayweather's era, it was his long-awaited showdown with Manny Pacquiao. For years, fans debated who was the best fighter of their generation, and negotiations for the bout dragged on for nearly six years due to disputes over drug testing, purse splits, and promotional conflicts. When the fight was finally announced for May 2, 2015, it became the most anticipated boxing match in decades.

The buildup was massive. Mayweather and Pacquiao were both multiple-division world champions, both had dominated their weight classes, and both had passionate fan bases. The fight was expected to be an all-out war between Mayweather's technical precision and Pacquiao's relentless offense.

However, once the bell rang, it was clear Mayweather had the perfect strategy. Using his superior defense, jab, and counterpunching, he neutralized Pacquiao's explosive combinations. While Pacquiao had some moments of success, Mayweather's ability to control the distance and dictate the pace of the fight led him to a unanimous decision victory.

The fight broke all financial records, generating over 4.6 million pay-per-view buys and grossing over $600 million. While some fans were disappointed by the lack of an all-out brawl, the fight solidified Mayweather's claim as the best boxer of his generation.

This bout was the pinnacle of his career—not just financially, but in terms of proving his style could conquer even the most aggressive and skilled opponent. It was the ultimate validation of Mayweather's mantra: "Hard work, dedication, and defense win fights."

Conclusion

Mayweather's biggest fights were not just about titles—they were moments that defined his legacy and reshaped boxing history. Whether it was his breakthrough against De La Hoya, his resilience against Mosley and Cotto, or the record-breaking showdown with Pacquiao, each bout contributed to his reputation as one of the greatest fighters of all time.

What made Mayweather unique was not just his ability to win, but the way he did it—with unmatched defensive skills, technical brilliance, and an understanding of boxing as both a sport and a business. His biggest fights weren't just about what happened inside the ring, but also about how they shaped the business of boxing, setting new financial standards and influencing future generations of fighters.

As we continue through his career, we'll see how Mayweather's approach to boxing extended beyond his undefeated record—into the very fabric of the sport itself.

Chapter 6: Controversies and Criticism

Floyd Mayweather Jr. is not just one of the greatest boxers of all time; he is also one of the most polarizing figures in sports history. His career has been defined by dominance in the ring, but outside of it, he has been embroiled in numerous controversies. Some see him as the ultimate businessman, a fighter who maximized his earning potential while taking minimal damage. Others view him as arrogant, calculating, and unwilling to take the risks that define true greatness.

This chapter delves into the key areas of controversy surrounding Mayweather—his legal issues and personal life, the public's perception of his persona, and the ongoing debate about his defensive, risk-averse fighting style.

Inside and Outside the Ring: Legal Issues and Personal Life

While Mayweather is celebrated for his discipline inside the ring, his personal life has been marred by numerous legal troubles. One of the most significant and recurring issues has been his history of domestic violence allegations.

In 2001, Mayweather faced two domestic violence charges, resulting in a six-month suspended sentence. Over the years, multiple accusations followed, the most serious being in 2010 when he was charged with domestic battery against Josie Harris, the mother of three of his children. He pleaded guilty in 2011 and served two months in jail. These incidents cast a shadow over his legacy, with critics arguing that his actions outside the ring should impact how he is viewed historically.

Despite these controversies, Mayweather has continued to thrive financially and professionally, with many of his fans and promoters downplaying or outright ignoring his legal troubles. However, his history with domestic violence has remained a point of contention, particularly among those who believe that athletes should be held accountable for their behavior outside their sport.

Beyond legal issues, Mayweather's lavish lifestyle has also drawn scrutiny. Known for his extravagant spending habits, he often flaunts his wealth on social media—posting stacks of cash, luxury cars, and expensive jewelry. While some see this as a testament to his success and financial intelligence, others criticize it as excessive and out of touch, especially considering his troubled past.

Despite all these personal controversies, Mayweather has largely remained unaffected in terms of career opportunities, continuing to secure massive paydays and global recognition.

Public Perception: Arrogance vs. Confidence

Mayweather is one of the most divisive figures in sports, with fans either admiring his confidence or despising what they see as arrogance. From early in his career, he cultivated an image that revolved around bravado, trash talk, and a relentless self-promotion strategy that made him both loved and hated.

His transformation from "Pretty Boy" Floyd to "Money" Mayweather was a calculated move that maximized his marketability. He embraced the role of the villain, understanding that people would pay just as much to see him lose as they would to see him win. His over-the-top personality, combined with his undefeated record, made him an icon of both success and controversy.

One of the key criticisms of Mayweather is that he has often belittled his opponents, boasting about his superiority and dismissing challengers. While this is a common tactic in combat sports, Mayweather's approach often went beyond typical pre-fight hype. His verbal assaults on fighters like Ricky Hatton, Manny Pacquiao, and Conor McGregor were not just competitive jabs but often deeply personal.

At the same time, his supporters argue that his confidence is well-earned. Unlike many athletes who fail to live up to their own hype, Mayweather backed up every claim he made in the ring. His perfectionism, discipline, and ability to mentally break down his opponents were part of what made him a generational talent.

Another aspect of his public perception is his relationship with the media. Mayweather has had contentious interactions with journalists, often refusing to engage with critics and dismissing tough questions about his legal issues or fighting style. This has further divided opinions about him, with some seeing it as a defensive mechanism and others viewing it as a lack of accountability.

Ultimately, the debate over Mayweather's personality comes down to perspective. Is he a confident champion who marketed himself brilliantly, or an arrogant figure who disrespected his opponents and evaded difficult questions? The answer depends on who you ask.

The Debate Over His Fighting Style

Perhaps the most enduring controversy in Mayweather's career is the debate over his fighting style. While purists and boxing analysts praise his defensive genius, critics argue that he avoided risk and prioritized winning over entertainment.

Mayweather's defensive mastery, particularly his use of the shoulder roll, has been studied and admired for years. His ability to evade punches, control the pace of a fight, and outthink opponents in real-time is what made him virtually untouchable in the ring. Unlike fighters who rely on brute strength or aggression, Mayweather's style was built on precision, patience, and efficiency.

However, this style also led to criticism. Some fans felt that Mayweather's fights lacked excitement compared to all-action brawlers like Manny Pacquiao or Canelo Álvarez. His ability to shut down aggressive fighters often resulted in less action-packed fights, with opponents struggling to land meaningful punches.

The criticism reached its peak after his fight with Pacquiao in 2015. Billed as the "Fight of the Century," the bout was expected to be an all-time classic. Instead, it was a tactical, defensive masterclass by Mayweather that left many casual fans disappointed. Pacquiao later claimed he had a shoulder injury, but the reality was that Mayweather had neutralized him using superior strategy. While boxing purists appreciated the performance, many fans and analysts felt the fight didn't live up to the hype.

Another point of contention is the accusation that Mayweather strategically picked his opponents at the right time. Critics argue that he avoided certain fighters when they were at their peak—such as Pacquiao earlier in his career—and only fought them when he believed they were declining. His supporters counter that Mayweather fought (and beat) every major challenger he faced, proving his greatness over a 20-year span.

Despite the criticism, it's undeniable that Mayweather's style was incredibly effective. He finished his career undefeated, a feat rarely seen in boxing, and made more money than any fighter in history. The debate over whether his style was "boring" or "brilliant" is likely to continue for years to come.

Conclusion

Floyd Mayweather's legacy is as complex as the man himself. Inside the ring, he was nearly flawless, demonstrating a level of skill and discipline unmatched in his era. Outside the ring, his legal troubles, flamboyant personality, and defensive fighting style have sparked ongoing debates.

What makes Mayweather fascinating is that he never sought to be universally loved—only respected. He embraced his role as the villain, used controversy to fuel his brand, and made himself the highest-paid athlete in the world. His approach to boxing, business, and fame was calculated and deliberate, ensuring that he remained at the top both financially and competitively.

Whether one views him as the greatest defensive boxer of all time or a fighter who avoided risk, his impact on the sport is undeniable. Mayweather's career is a testament to the power of strategy—both inside the ring and outside of it.

Chapter 7: The Business of Floyd Mayweather

Floyd Mayweather Jr. is not just one of the greatest boxers in history—he is also one of the most successful businessmen in sports. While his undefeated record is a testament to his skill in the ring, his ability to maximize his financial success outside of it is what truly sets him apart. He understood early on that boxing was not just about winning fights—it was about controlling the business, branding himself as a global icon, and ensuring that every fight was an event that generated massive revenue.

This chapter explores how Mayweather built his brand, the financial strategies that helped him become boxing's first billionaire, and the lasting impact of The Money Team (TMT) as a business empire.

Building the Mayweather Brand

Floyd Mayweather's transformation from a young, skilled boxer into a global brand was not accidental—it was a carefully executed plan. From his early days as "Pretty Boy" Floyd to his reinvention as "Money" Mayweather, he understood the power of image, marketing, and controversy.

One of the most significant moments in Mayweather's business journey was his decision to leave Top Rank Promotions, the company that managed his early career. In 2006, Mayweather bought himself out of his contract for $750,000, a move that many saw as risky. However, it turned out to be one of the best business decisions in boxing history. By becoming his own promoter, he took full control over his earnings, fight negotiations, and career trajectory.

Mayweather also embraced the role of the villain. Unlike traditional fan-favorite fighters who built their brands on humility or charisma, he marketed himself as the man people loved to hate. He flaunted his wealth, talked trash, and positioned himself as the ultimate winner. This persona made people tune in—whether they wanted to see him win or lose, they paid to watch.

His business model revolved around creating massive events rather than just boxing matches. Every fight became a spectacle, complete with world tours, heated press conferences, and extravagant entrances. He turned his career into a reality show, leveraging social media to keep fans engaged and invested in his every move.

Through these strategies, Mayweather transformed himself into more than just a boxer—he became a brand.

Money Moves: How He Became Boxing's First Billionaire

Mayweather's ability to generate wealth was unprecedented in boxing. Unlike many fighters who rely on promoters to handle their earnings, Mayweather ensured that he controlled every aspect of the financial side of his career.

One of the biggest factors in his financial success was his pay-per-view (PPV) strategy. Under his promotional company, Mayweather Promotions, he negotiated deals that allowed him to take a percentage of PPV sales rather than a flat fight purse. This meant that instead of simply earning a set amount for a fight, he earned a share of the total revenue generated.

His fight against Oscar De La Hoya in 2007 was a turning point. The fight generated 2.4 million PPV buys, making it the most lucrative boxing match at the time. Mayweather earned around $25 million for the fight, proving that he could be the biggest draw in the sport.

From there, his earnings skyrocketed:

- Mayweather vs. Canelo Álvarez (2013): Generated $150 million in revenue, with Mayweather earning over $70 million.
- Mayweather vs. Manny Pacquiao (2015): Shattered records with 4.6 million PPV buys and over $600 million in total revenue. Mayweather took home approximately $250 million from this fight alone.

- Mayweather vs. Conor McGregor (2017): A crossover event that brought in over $550 million in revenue, with Mayweather earning at least $275 million.

Beyond PPV earnings, Mayweather leveraged sponsorships, merchandise sales, and international exhibition fights to continue generating wealth. Even after his official retirement, he participated in high-profile exhibition bouts, including fights in Japan and the Middle East, where he reportedly earned tens of millions for short bouts against non-traditional opponents.

His financial discipline, despite his extravagant spending, has also been a key factor in maintaining his wealth. While Mayweather is known for his luxury cars, private jets, and multi-million-dollar mansions, he is also known for smart investments in real estate, business ventures, and maintaining control over his brand.

Through these strategies, Mayweather became boxing's first billionaire, proving that financial intelligence is just as important as talent in building a lasting legacy.

The Legacy of The Money Team (TMT)

One of Mayweather's most significant business ventures has been the creation of The Money Team (TMT)—a brand that extends beyond boxing and into lifestyle, fashion, and business.

TMT started as Mayweather's inner circle, a group of close friends and associates who traveled with him and represented his brand. However, it soon evolved into a full-fledged business empire, with its own merchandise, promotional company, and fighter management division.

Mayweather turned TMT into a recognizable symbol of wealth, success, and hustle. The brand's merchandise—including hats, shirts, and accessories—became a staple among fans and celebrities alike. By leveraging his own influence and the power of social media, Mayweather turned TMT into a profitable fashion and lifestyle brand.

Mayweather Promotions

Mayweather Promotions is one of the most successful boxing promotional companies, managing fighters and hosting major events. Unlike traditional promoters who take large percentages of a fighter's earnings, Mayweather built a model where fighters have more control over their financial success, similar to how he managed his own career.

Several notable fighters have been under the Mayweather Promotions banner, including:

- Gervonta "Tank" Davis – A young knockout artist seen as the future of boxing.
- Badou Jack – A former world champion who found success under Mayweather's guidance.

By creating his own promotional company, Mayweather ensured that he remained influential in the boxing world even after his retirement.

Investments and Business Ventures

Beyond boxing, Mayweather has made smart business moves in real estate, nightclub ownership, and various investment opportunities. He has consistently emphasized financial independence and has used his platform to educate younger athletes about managing their earnings wisely.

Despite criticisms that he spends lavishly, Mayweather has demonstrated that his wealth is built on long-term financial strategies, ensuring that he remains one of the richest athletes even years after retiring from competitive boxing.

Conclusion

Floyd Mayweather's business acumen is just as impressive as his boxing skills. He understood that boxing was not just about being the best fighter—it was about being the smartest businessman. From taking control of his promotional deals to maximizing pay-per-view revenue, he built a financial empire that no other boxer has matched.

The Mayweather brand, fueled by The Money Team, continues to thrive as a representation of success, hustle, and financial independence. His journey from a young fighter in Grand Rapids to a self-made billionaire is a testament to his vision, discipline, and understanding of both sports and business.

Mayweather's story is not just about boxing—it's about strategy, branding, and making calculated moves that ensure long-term success. Whether one admires or criticizes him, his impact on the business side of sports is undeniable. His legacy as a fighter will always be debated, but his influence as a businessman is unquestionable.

Chapter 8: Life Beyond Boxing

Floyd Mayweather Jr. has never been just a boxer—he's a brand, a businessman, and a master strategist. His career inside the ring was defined by dominance, precision, and an undefeated record, but what truly sets him apart is his ability to remain relevant and financially successful long after most fighters fade into obscurity. Unlike many boxing greats who struggled post-retirement, Mayweather carefully orchestrated his exit from professional competition while ensuring that his name and earnings continued to thrive.

In this chapter, we will explore Mayweather's life beyond competitive boxing, examining his multiple retirement announcements and comebacks, his lucrative exhibition fights, and his expansive business ventures that have solidified his wealth and influence.

Retirement Announcements and Comebacks

Mayweather's career has been marked by multiple retirements, each generating speculation about whether he would truly step away from the sport. His retirements were never just quiet exits; they were grand narratives that built anticipation and demand for his return.

First Retirement (2007)

Following his victory over Oscar De La Hoya and his subsequent stoppage win against Ricky Hatton, Mayweather shocked the boxing world in June 2008 by announcing his retirement. At just 30 years old and at the peak of his career, many questioned whether he was truly done. However, this was more of a strategic move than a true farewell. By stepping away, he created intrigue and increased his value for an eventual comeback.

The Comeback (2009)

In 2009, Mayweather returned to the ring to fight Juan Manuel Márquez. His comeback was heavily marketed as the return of the king, drawing massive pay-per-view sales. His victory over Márquez re-established him as the biggest name in boxing, setting up future mega-fights.

Retirement After Pacquiao and Berto (2015)

After finally facing and defeating Manny Pacquiao in 2015—one of the most anticipated fights in history—Mayweather announced his retirement following a victory over Andre Berto. At 49-0, he claimed he had nothing left to prove. Many believed this was his final exit from the sport.

The McGregor Fight and "Final" Retirement (2017)

Two years later, Mayweather returned for a once-in-a-lifetime crossover bout against UFC star Conor McGregor. The fight, although criticized by purists, was a financial blockbuster, earning Mayweather an estimated $275 million. After this victory, he retired again with a perfect 50-0 record.

However, true to form, he never completely walked away from the ring. Instead of traditional fights, he transitioned into exhibition bouts, allowing him to continue earning massive paydays while maintaining his legacy.

Exhibition Fights and Staying Relevant

Mayweather found a way to remain relevant in boxing while avoiding the dangers of full-fledged professional bouts. His entry into exhibition fights allowed him to capitalize on his star power without the same level of physical risk.

Mayweather vs. Tenshin Nasukawa (2018)

In 2018, Mayweather fought Japanese kickboxer Tenshin Nasukawa in an exhibition match in Tokyo. The fight lasted less than one round, as Mayweather easily dominated his much smaller opponent. Despite its brevity, the event reportedly earned him $9 million for just a few minutes of work.

Mayweather vs. Logan Paul (2021)

One of the most talked-about exhibitions in recent history was Mayweather's match against YouTube star Logan Paul. Despite criticism that the fight was more spectacle than sport, it attracted millions of viewers. While no official winner was declared, Mayweather reportedly made around $100 million from the event.

Other Exhibitions and Future Fights

Mayweather has continued to accept exhibition fights, including bouts against mixed martial artists and influencers in various global markets. These fights allow him to maintain public interest, keep The Money Team brand active, and generate substantial revenue without the high stakes of professional boxing.

His ability to adapt to modern entertainment trends—such as influencer boxing and social media hype—has kept him relevant among younger generations. While many retired fighters struggle to stay in the spotlight, Mayweather has embraced the entertainment era, proving that his business acumen extends beyond traditional boxing.

Business Ventures and Investments

One of the most remarkable aspects of Mayweather's post-boxing life is his ability to maintain and grow his wealth. While many athletes go bankrupt after retirement, Mayweather has expanded his business empire through smart investments and strategic branding.

Mayweather Promotions

Mayweather Promotions, his boxing promotional company, remains a powerhouse in the industry. Unlike traditional promoters who take a large percentage of a fighter's earnings, Mayweather provides fighters with more control over their finances.

Notable fighters under Mayweather Promotions include:

- Gervonta "Tank" Davis – A rising star in boxing and one of the sport's biggest knockout artists.
- Badou Jack – A multi-division world champion.

By promoting young talent, Mayweather ensures that his name remains relevant in the boxing business, even as he no longer competes professionally.

Real Estate Investments

Mayweather has invested heavily in real estate, owning multiple properties across the United States. He has emphasized the importance of passive income, stating that he makes millions every month from his real estate portfolio.

His luxury properties include:

- A multi-million-dollar mansion in Las Vegas
- A Beverly Hills estate worth over $25 million
- Various commercial properties and apartment complexes

Unlike some athletes who waste their earnings on depreciating assets, Mayweather has ensured that a significant portion of his wealth is tied to long-term investments.

The Money Team (TMT) Brand

The Money Team (TMT) has become more than just a slogan—it's a fully operational brand that includes:

- Clothing and merchandise sales

- Business partnerships and sponsorships
- A lifestyle movement associated with wealth, success, and luxury

TMT's merchandise, particularly its hats and apparel, has been widely embraced by fans and celebrities alike, generating significant revenue.

Nightclubs and Entertainment Businesses

Mayweather has also ventured into the nightlife industry, owning businesses such as Girl Collection, a high-end gentleman's club in Las Vegas. His involvement in entertainment ventures further cements his status as a businessman beyond sports.

Conclusion

Floyd Mayweather's life beyond boxing has been a masterclass in financial planning, branding, and strategic reinvention. Unlike many fighters who struggle to adapt after retirement, Mayweather has remained a dominant force in sports and entertainment.

Through exhibition fights, he continues to generate massive paydays while avoiding the physical risks of professional bouts. His business ventures, from Mayweather Promotions to real estate and TMT branding, have ensured that his wealth continues to grow.

Perhaps his greatest achievement is proving that a fighter doesn't have to fade away after retiring. He has shown that boxing is not just about what happens inside the ring—it's about controlling your narrative, owning your brand, and making smart financial decisions.

Mayweather's post-boxing journey is a blueprint for athletes who aspire to maintain relevance and financial success long after their prime. Whether admired or criticized, his impact on sports and business is undeniable.

Chapter 9: Mayweather's Legacy in Boxing

Floyd Mayweather Jr.'s impact on boxing extends far beyond his undefeated record. His influence reshaped the sport both financially and technically, setting new standards for how fighters approach business, strategy, and training. While comparisons to boxing's all-time greats are inevitable, what sets Mayweather apart is his ability to combine skill, intelligence, and business acumen to redefine the game.

In this chapter, we will analyze Mayweather's lasting legacy—how he changed the sport from both a financial and technical standpoint, how he stacks up against the greatest boxers in history, and how his influence is evident in the next generation of fighters.

How He Changed the Sport Financially and Technically

The Business of Boxing: Fighter Control Over Earnings

Before Mayweather, most boxers were at the mercy of promoters and networks, earning a fraction of the money generated from their fights. Mayweather changed this by taking complete control of his career. He negotiated his own deals, cut out traditional promoters, and ensured that he received the lion's share of the revenue.

- Pay-Per-View King: Mayweather's fights generated more than $1.6 billion in PPV revenue, surpassing legends like Mike Tyson and Evander Holyfield. His ability to sell fights, whether as the hero or villain, set a new benchmark.

- Largest Payouts in History: He earned an estimated $275 million from the McGregor fight and $250 million from the Pacquiao fight, making him the highest-paid athlete in multiple years.
- TMT Model: By promoting himself through Mayweather Promotions, he maximized his earnings while maintaining ownership of his brand, influencing fighters like Canelo Álvarez and Gervonta "Tank" Davis to follow suit.

The Technical Revolution: Defense Over Offense

Mayweather's technical approach revolutionized modern boxing. In an era where knockout artists were celebrated, he proved that defense wins fights.

- The Shoulder Roll Defense: Borrowing from old-school boxers like James Toney, Mayweather perfected the shoulder roll, using it to deflect punches while remaining in a counter-punching position.
- Ring IQ and Adaptability: Unlike many fighters who rely on physical attributes, Mayweather's ability to analyze opponents and adjust mid-fight made him nearly impossible to beat. His strategic dismantling of aggressive punchers like Canelo Álvarez and Ricky Hatton demonstrated his boxing intelligence.
- Punch Accuracy and Efficiency: Mayweather rarely wasted punches. In many fights, his accuracy exceeded 50%, while his opponents often landed below 20%. His fight against Canelo Álvarez showcased a

masterclass in efficiency, where he landed 46% of his punches compared to Canelo's 22%.

His defensive style, once criticized as "boring," is now widely respected as the gold standard for longevity in boxing.

Comparing Mayweather to Boxing's All-Time Greats

Mayweather's place in boxing history is a subject of debate. Many consider him one of the best, if not the best, while others argue that he avoided certain challenges to protect his record.

Undefeated vs. The Legends

One of Mayweather's greatest claims is his 50-0 record, surpassing Rocky Marciano's 49-0. However, some critics argue that an undefeated record alone doesn't define greatness—quality of opponents and dominance matter just as much.

Here's how he compares to other all-time greats:

- Muhammad Ali (56-5): Ali fought in a tougher heavyweight era, facing killers like Joe Frazier, George Foreman, and Sonny Liston. His willingness to take risks, engage in wars, and fight through adversity (such as the Thrilla in Manila) sets him apart.

- Sugar Ray Robinson (173-19-6): Considered by many the greatest pound-for-pound fighter ever, Robinson's mix of power, speed, and durability made him unbeatable in his prime. However, he fought far more often than Mayweather, sometimes multiple times a month.
- Sugar Ray Leonard (36-3-1): Leonard's resume includes victories over Roberto Durán, Thomas Hearns, and Marvin Hagler—fighters considered among the best in multiple weight classes.

Strengths of Mayweather's Case for GOAT Status

- Longevity and Dominance: Unlike Ali or Leonard, Mayweather was never seriously hurt or knocked down in his career. His ability to control fights and win decisively, even against prime champions like Canelo and Diego Corrales, is unmatched.
- Skill Mastery: While Ali relied on speed and reflexes and Robinson on knockout power, Mayweather's mastery of the sweet science—hitting without getting hit—demonstrated a level of control few have ever achieved.
- Fighter IQ and Adaptability: Mayweather neutralized all styles. He dismantled sluggers, outclassed technical boxers, and frustrated

power punchers. His fights against Juan Manuel Márquez and Manny Pacquiao showed his ability to adjust against elite competition.

Criticism Against Mayweather's Legacy

- Lack of Risk-Taking: Unlike Ali, who took on Foreman and Frazier in grueling battles, or Leonard, who fought wars against Hall of Famers, Mayweather's strategic matchmaking ensured he always had an advantage.
- Avoiding Certain Fighters in Their Primes: Critics argue that he fought Pacquiao too late (2015 instead of 2010) and avoided tough opponents like Paul Williams and Antonio Margarito in their peak years.
- Defensive Style Perception: While purists appreciate his defense, casual

fans often found his fights less entertaining than those of knockout artists like Tyson or Julio César Chávez.

Despite these criticisms, Mayweather's ability to remain undefeated while facing elite opposition is a testament to his greatness.

Influence on the Next Generation of Fighters

Mayweather's impact isn't just about his own success—his influence is seen in today's biggest stars.

Fighters Who Emulate Mayweather's Style

- Shakur Stevenson & Devin Haney: Both young stars have adopted Mayweather's defensive-first approach, using movement and precision to dominate opponents. Stevenson, in particular, has drawn comparisons to a young Floyd with his slick counterpunching and ring control.
- Gervonta "Tank" Davis: As a protégé of Mayweather, Davis has absorbed elements of Floyd's fight promotion

and defensive skills but combines them with knockout power.
- Terence Crawford: While more aggressive than Mayweather, Crawford's ability to make mid-fight adjustments mirrors Floyd's adaptability.

Business Influence: Fighters Taking Control of Their Careers

- Canelo Álvarez: After losing to Mayweather, Canelo adopted his own version of the TMT model, negotiating massive fight deals with DAZN and securing financial independence.
- Ryan Garcia & The YouTube Era: Mayweather's ability to promote himself outside traditional boxing channels has influenced social media-driven fighters like Ryan

Garcia, Jake Paul, and KSI, who leverage entertainment and business acumen to maximize earnings.

The Defensive Revolution

Before Mayweather, defensive boxing was often overshadowed by knockout artists. Today, more fighters focus on movement, counterpunching, and hit-and-don't-get-hit strategies, proving his technical impact on the sport.

Conclusion

Floyd Mayweather's legacy is undeniable. Financially, he changed the sport forever, showing fighters how to take control of their earnings and brand themselves beyond boxing. Technically, he mastered defense and efficiency, setting a new gold standard for longevity and ring intelligence.

While debates will continue about his place among the all-time greats, his influence on modern boxing is unquestionable. Future generations of fighters are not only emulating his style but also following his blueprint for career control and financial success.

Whether loved or hated, Mayweather redefined boxing—and that, more than any undefeated record, is his true legacy.

Chapter 10: What It Means to Be Undefeated

Floyd Mayweather Jr.'s 50-0 record is more than just an achievement in boxing—it's a testament to his mentality, discipline, and relentless pursuit of perfection. In a sport where one mistake can cost a career, Mayweather remained undefeated, outlasting every opponent who stood in front of him.

But what does it truly mean to be undefeated? Beyond the numbers, it's about mindset, sacrifice, and the ability to adapt under pressure. In this chapter, we'll explore the mentality of a champion, the price of perfection, and the lessons that can be drawn from Mayweather's career, both inside and outside the ring.

The Mentality of a Champion

Mayweather's success wasn't just about physical ability—it was rooted in a mindset that refused to accept anything less than greatness.

The Will to Win

Mayweather approached every fight with an unshakable belief in himself. Unlike some fighters who rely on sheer aggression or brute force, his victories were built on intelligence, patience, and meticulous planning.

- Confidence, Not Cockiness: While Mayweather's bravado was often mistaken for arrogance, it was a necessary tool for his success. In his mind, there was no doubt that he was the best, and this unwavering

self-belief translated into dominance in the ring.
- Mind Games and Psychological Warfare: Mayweather didn't just defeat opponents physically—he broke them mentally. His trash talk and mind games before fights, whether against Oscar De La Hoya, Ricky Hatton, or Conor McGregor, put pressure on his rivals before they even stepped into the ring.

The Art of Preparation

Mayweather's training camps were legendary. He outworked his opponents not just during fights but in the months leading up to them.

- Sparring Smarter, Not Harder: Instead of absorbing unnecessary damage in training, Mayweather focused on sharpening reflexes, footwork, and defensive maneuvers.

- Unmatched Work Ethic: Stories of Mayweather running at 3 AM or training immediately after a fight became part of his mythos. His mantra, "Hard work, dedication," wasn't just a slogan—it was a way of life.

Mayweather's mental toughness made him virtually untouchable in the ring. His ability to stay composed under pressure, adapt to any opponent, and execute a fight plan flawlessly is what separated him from the rest.

The Price of Perfection: Sacrifices and Discipline

Remaining undefeated isn't just about skill—it requires immense sacrifices. Mayweather's perfection came at a cost, both personally and professionally.

Discipline Over Everything

Mayweather was never the biggest, strongest, or hardest-hitting fighter. His advantage came from his discipline.

- No Off-Season Mentality: While other fighters took long breaks, Mayweather maintained a near-constant state of training. Even in retirement, he kept himself in shape, ready for any opportunity.
- Strict Diet and Lifestyle: Unlike many boxers who balloon in weight

between fights, Mayweather stayed within striking distance of his fight weight year-round. His ability to make weight effortlessly gave him an edge.

- Avoiding Unnecessary Damage: One of the reasons Mayweather retired without significant physical decline was his defensive approach. He avoided punishing fights that shortened careers and stayed disciplined in the ring.

Personal Sacrifices

The quest for perfection often comes with personal costs. Mayweather's life revolved around boxing, sometimes at the expense of personal relationships.

- Strained Friendships and Family Tensions: His single-minded pursuit of greatness sometimes put distance between him and loved ones. His relationship with his father and trainer, Floyd Mayweather Sr., was tumultuous, though ultimately reconciled.

- Criticism and Scrutiny: The same persona that made him a superstar also made him one of the most polarizing figures in sports. Constant media scrutiny, legal troubles, and controversies followed him throughout his career.

The Pressure to Stay Undefeated

In boxing, an undefeated record is rare. The pressure to maintain it can be suffocating.

- High-Stakes Fights: Every fight Mayweather took was a must-win. Unlike other greats who could afford a loss and bounce back, Mayweather had no such luxury.

- Strategic Fight Selection: Critics argue that Mayweather sometimes played it safe, picking opponents at the right time. Whether this was smart business or a cautious approach to preserving his record remains a topic of debate.

Despite these sacrifices, Mayweather never cracked under pressure. His ability to thrive in the most intense moments is what defined his greatness.

Lessons from Mayweather's Career

Mayweather's undefeated career offers valuable lessons—not just for athletes but for anyone striving for success in their own field.

1. Master Your Craft

Mayweather didn't become the best by accident. He dedicated decades to perfecting his skills, studying opponents, and refining his technique.

- Lesson: Whatever your field, mastery takes time. Study, practice, and continuously improve.

2. Work Smarter, Not Just Harder

Many fighters trained hard, but Mayweather trained smart. He understood the importance of longevity and efficiency.

- Lesson: Hard work is essential, but strategy and precision matter just as much. Avoid burnout by working intelligently.

3. Bet on Yourself

Mayweather took financial control of his career, ensuring that he—not promoters—reaped the rewards of his success.

- Lesson: In business and life, don't be afraid to take control of your own destiny. If you believe in your worth, don't settle for less.

4. Defense Wins Championships

Mayweather's style wasn't always exciting to casual fans, but it was effective. His ability to avoid damage extended his career and ensured he left the sport on his own terms.

- Lesson: Whether in sports, business, or life, risk management is key. Sometimes, playing it smart is better than going all-out recklessly.

5. Mental Strength is Everything

Mayweather never doubted himself. He visualized success, embraced pressure, and never let negativity shake his confidence.

- Lesson: The right mindset can make or break you. Confidence, resilience, and self-belief are crucial for long-term success.

Conclusion

Being undefeated isn't just about numbers—it's a mindset, a lifestyle, and a commitment to excellence. Mayweather's 50-0 record isn't just a statistic; it's a reflection of decades of discipline, sacrifice, and unparalleled mental toughness.

His legacy goes beyond boxing. Whether admired or criticized, Mayweather showed what it takes to remain at the top without ever tasting defeat. His journey offers lessons that extend beyond the ring, teaching us about mastery, discipline, self-confidence, and the importance of controlling one's own destiny.

In the end, Floyd Mayweather Jr. didn't just win fights—he redefined what it means to be undefeated